MW00364362

The Eye of The Needle

And Other Prophetic Parables

by

Dr. E. Charlotte Baker

Copyright

Parable
Publications

Parable Publications is a ministry The McDougal
Foundation, Inc., a nonprofit Maryland Corpora-
tion dedicated to spreading the Gospel of the Lord
Jesus Christ to as many people as possible in the
shortest time possible.

Published by:

Parable Publications
P.O. Box 3595
Hagerstown, MD 21742-3595
www.mcdougal.org

ISBN 1-884369-62-6

1st Printing 1997
2nd Printing June 1999

Printed in the United States of America
For Worldwide Distribution

Dedication

This book is affectionately dedicated to my dear and faithful friend, Dr. David E. Schoch of Benbrook, Texas, whose ministry and friendship have so greatly enriched my life.

To Dr. Ione Glaeser,
my friend:

Through the years we shared so much together –
our joys and our burdens, our laughter and our
tears; but best of all we shared the wonders of
God's Word.

Thank you, Ione, for the fun, the laughter and all
the pleasures we enjoyed. Thank you for always
being there with your loyalty and encouragement
when I ministered, and as I present these parables
for publishing, I am very grateful, and I only wish
you could be here to share my joy.

Thank you for being my friend. I miss you.

– *Char*

Acknowledgments

My sister, Julia Martin, spent many long hours working on this manuscript, and for her loyal service I am especially grateful.

Special thanks also to my Gates of Praise family and their pastor, Debbie Lynch, for all of their encouragement, prayers and financial help during the time of the preparation of this manuscript.

Contents

Author's Preface 9

Introduction 11

1. The Parable of The Master Musician 13
2. The Parable of The Wounded Tree 19
3. The Parable of The Wasted Years 27
4. The Parable of The Secret of Greatness 35
5. The Parable of The Beggar in King's
   Clothes 41
6. The Parable of The Solitary Man 47
7. The Parable of The Kingdom 55
8. The Parable of The Seasons 63
9. The Parable of The Wind 71
10. The Parable of The High Places 79
11. The Parable of The Snow 87
12. The Parable of The Way of Peace 95
13. The Parable of The Worshiping Shepherd . 101
14. The Parable of The Broken Heart 109
15. The Parable of The High Road 115
16. The Parable of The Eye of the Needle 125

To the chief Musician, A Psalm for the sons of Korah. Hear this, all ye people; give ear, all ye inhabitants of the world: Both low and high, rich and poor, together. My mouth shall speak of wisdom; and the meditation of my heart shall be of understanding. I WILL INCLINE MINE EAR TO A PARABLE: I will open my dark saying upon the harp.   Psalm 49:1-4

Author's Preface

Much of the teaching which our Lord Jesus Christ gave when He was on Earth was clothed in parables. To the Scribes and Pharisees, this brought constant confusion, but to Jesus' disciples it was a vehicle through which the Holy Spirit could reveal the deep truths and principles of the Kingdom.

God is still speaking to His people in parables, for many of the precious truths revealed to this generation are being found hidden in the teaching of parables. They are hidden, that is, until the Holy Spirit seeks to reveal them to the Church.

No prophecy is given to "prove" or "confirm" the Word of God, rather God has given His Word to confirm and prove each prophetic utterance. God's Spirit, in no way, provokes spiritual utterances which step outside the written Word.

The realm of prophetic parables is a vehicle which God is restoring to His Church in this last hour for the purpose of revealing present truth.

With these thoughts in mind, we have undertaken to put into print some of the prophetic parables God has given over the past years to various congregations and conferences. These parables are often given in the first person, as they have not only been spoken, but also experienced in the Spirit by the one speaking forth the parable.

Introduction

The prophetic parables you are about to read were birthed in the anointing. They were in no way rehearsed or pre-planned, but rather came forth in a completely spontaneous way, as the result of a peculiar special anointing of the Holy Spirit, a mantle which falls upon me during times of deep worship. At such times I lose all sense of my natural surroundings and am caught up in God's presence to a sacred place made known to me as "the Circle of the Earth." There, in a heavenly atmosphere, earthly things cease to exist and only the eternal is real.

It is my deep heart's cry that these parables will be life-changing for you, as you allow God to make eternal values real to your heart.

Dr. E. Charlotte Baker

And I saw as it were a sea of glass mingled with fire: and them that had gotten the victory over the beast, and over his image, and over his mark, and over the number of his name, stand on the sea of glass, having the harps of God. And they sing the song of Moses the servant of God, and the song of the Lamb, saying, Great and marvellous are thy works, Lord God Almighty; just and true are thy ways, thou King of saints. Who shall not fear thee, O Lord, and glorify thy name? for thou only art holy: for all nations shall come and worship before thee; for thy judgments are made manifest.

Revelation 15:2-4

Chapter One

The Parable of
The Master Musician

ON A CERTAIN DAY I HEARD the Word of the Lord speak unto me, "Come up higher, son of man, for I have somewhat to say unto thee, and when I speak unto thee, thou shalt speak unto My people, for it is time that My people tuned their ear to hear the Word of their God."

As I stood upon the Circle of the Earth, the Lord opened my eyes, and I saw a strange sight. The Master Musician called for His instruments. As the instruments presented themselves before the Master, He first called forth the wind instruments, and then He spoke to them, and He said, "Wind, blow upon these instruments."

As He blew and blew upon these instruments, they said within themselves, "The Master blows upon us, and we make a good sound."

They made sound after sound, and the Master Musician looked at them, and He said, "Stop! No more! For though the wind blows, and though the sound comes, it is only a sound that pleases the ears of men, and I have called thee, oh thou instruments, that when I blow upon thee, thou wilt make a sound that will please the King."

The instruments bowed low at the feet of the Master Musician, and they said, "Tune us, tune us, tune us, tune us, for we would no longer make a sound that pleases men, but we would make a sound that is fit for the King."

Once again the Master Musician stood before His instruments, and He called forth the strings, and He said, "Come before me and play." The strings began to play, and they played a wonderful sound. They played happy music, and they played quiet music. They played skillfully, and their strings made a wonderful sound.

The Master Musician lifted His voice, and He said, "Enough! Enough! Play no more, but come to Me, for I would stretch thee yet again."

The Parable of The Master Musician

The strings said, "O, Master, what art thou doing to us, for we make a sound that is pleasing in the ears of men?"

He answered, "It is not enough until thou art stretched again to make thee pleasing in the ears of the King."

The strings came and presented themselves, and the Master Musician stretched and he stretched, tighter and tighter and tighter until, when the strings played again, the sound was pleasing to the ears of the King.

The Master Musician called forth those who played on the drums, and they began to play on their drums, and they made a wonderful military sound of war, and they played as men marched before them, and their sound was great and glorious, and men said, "Surely these drums make a wonderful sound."

The Master Musician lifted His hand again, and He said, "No more! No more! For thou dost make only the sound of war. I will come now, and I will stretch thine skins and touch thine mallets, until thy sound of war no longer finds an echo in the hearts of men. It shall be, instead, the sound of glorious cadence that moves the heart of the King. Surely then thou shalt be a sound in the ears of the King."

Now hear this, ye people. I have been pleased

with that which thou hast presented to this point. It hath been wonderful, it hath been good, and the God Whom thou dost love and serve and for Whom thou hast given thy life has looked upon thee and said, "That is a good sound, and I am glad that thou art pleasing unto My people, but I will do a new work within thee, for surely I will blow upon this people again," saith the Lord, "this time not to make thee more skillful in the ears and eyes of men, but to make thee more pleasing in My sight."

"I will blow and blow and blow upon thee until, when thou dost go from this place, thou shalt return to thine own place and say, 'My God hath blown upon me,' and thou wilt say one to another, 'My God hath stretched me beyond what I thought I could be stretched, and surely, when He hath stretched me and stretched me, I shall no longer only be pleasing to men, and no longer will I minister unto them alone, but I will minister unto my God.' "

As the Word of the Lord came, He lifted me again to the Circle of the Earth, and He said, "Come one more time, and I will show thee what I do."

Surely this time the Master Musician called the wind instruments, and He called the string instruments, and He called the percussions, and He called the dancers, and He called all of those who ministered in the House of the Lord. He said, "This time, a new thing has come upon this people, for I blow upon the instruments and they play. I speak to the strings and they sing. I speak to percussion and it makes not only a sound of war, but a sound of majesty in the presence of the King. If thou wilt present thyself, this day, before thy God, I will do this thing."

Therefore, strings, begin to play. Therefore, wind instruments, begin to blow. Yea, percussion, begin to make a sound. Dancers, begin to dance like thou hast never danced before, and the King shall come and sit among thee.

The wilderness and the solitary place shall be glad for them; and the desert shall rejoice, and blossom as the rose. It shall blossom abundantly, and rejoice even with joy and singing: the glory of Lebanon shall be given unto it, the excellency of Carmel and Sharon, they shall see the glory of the LORD, and the excellency of our God. **Isaiah 35:1-2**

Chapter Two

The Parable of
The Wounded Tree

THERE WAS A DAY IN MY youth when I stood strong as an oak tree in the presence of my God. I said within myself, "God has given me much and made me great, and I stand among the trees of the wood, taller than most, and stronger than most." I saw as the winds blew through my branches, that while the leaves of other trees fell, mine hung on, and I was strong, and I was filled with life. I lifted my hands before my God, and I said, "God, in me Thou hast done a good thing."

My heart rejoiced as I, looking around, saw the Great Master of the trees coming through the woods. He went to one and looked at it, and He said, "Thou art a good tree, and I will dig about thee, and I will dung thee, and I will prune thee, that thou become a better tree." He said this to many trees, and then He did a strange thing. He went through the forest of trees, and He pulled from His side a sharp knife, and He cut the bark of a tree. I saw as, one after another, He cut the bark of others.

I said, "This is not my God. Why would my God do this? He cuts the very heart of a tree until the life will bleed out of that tree." I dropped to my knees, and I said, "Something is wrong here," and I drew myself in, and I said, "I hope He comes not near me, for I am fearful of what this husbandman will do." Surely, He walked straight to me, and He took in His hand the knife, and He cut me to the very heart. I felt the piercing, and I felt life begin to flow from me, and I began to wonder at such a thing.

When I looked at that which He had carved, I saw that it was His name that He had carved upon my tree. My heart leaped within me, and I said, "O God, I stand again strong and tall in Thy presence, for Thou has put upon me Thy name."

I rejoiced for a season, and then the wind began to blow, and I heard the voice of the Lord say, "Every time the wind blows it is a sign that change is coming. Be thou prepared for change, for as I have put My name upon thee, so have I also destined thee for change."

Again, I said, "I can take it; I am strong. Though I have a scar, I am still strong."

On a certain day, when the wind had blown ferociously, and the fierceness of the elements had come upon me, I heard footsteps behind me, and I looked, and there came that same Husbandman, and my heart fell. I said, "Well, He cometh only to bless me, only to promote me, only to make me great among the trees of the wood, for I am stronger than most and taller than most, and I have been cut by the sword, and I bear His name." However, when He came closer I saw that He had, this time, not a knife, but He had an axe. Again, I recoiled at the awful thought that He might use that axe on me.

As He walked among the trees of the wood, He looked until He saw one that was me, and He took the axe and, with great fervor and with great joy, He cut the tree down. I saw joy on His face, and I said, "This I cannot understand. I cannot understand why He would take a tree and cut it to the roots." But when I fell, I fell in His presence.

He took the axe, and He cut me where no man had ever touched me, and He hollowed out the very center of my being. I wept like I had never wept before and begged Him to stay His hand, for the pain and the bruising and the hurting was more than I thought I could bear, and I began to cry, "Stay Thy hand, O God. Is it not enough that Thou hast felled me in the presence of my friends? Is it not enough that Thou hast wounded me? Is it not enough that when my friends are standing upright I must lay low, even if I am in Thy presence?"

But He kept right on working until He was satisfied, until He had seen the travail of His soul, and then He did a beautiful thing. He picked me up, and He put me on His shoulder, and together we went out of the forest, away from my friends. My heart said, "O, now He doeth it to me again. I will have no friends. I will be taken away from those I love and from the fellowship to which I am joined."

The Word of the Lord came unto me, "I want thee to come to the Circle of the Earth, for up there is where I hold the wind in My fist, where I speak the clouds into their directions, where I cause the snow to fall and the sun to shine. Up there, on the Circle of the Earth, I would speak unto thee, son of man. Thou wast not born to be a tree that was taller and greater, nor wast thou only born to be one who bears the scars of My name, but thou art one who was born to be My possession. I have come to do with thee whatsoever My heart desires. It is not my desire that thou bloom among the trees. It is My desire that thou come with Me to a high place."

Again He brought me down, and I saw myself upon the shoulders of the Husbandman, and He crawled over the rocks, and He crawled into barren places and up tc the high mountain, and I said, "Now this is terrible, there is nobody here, there is nothing here. What can I do? O, woe is me, I will be alone."

The voice of the Lord said, "Alone? How canst thou be alone on a high place, because I dwell in the high places?"

When He found a little stream, He laid me gently down, and He put me into that stream, and suddenly that stream became a great river.

The Lord spoke again to me and said, "Now come, and I shall give thee the parable of the tree." He took me to the Circle of the Earth, and He said, "Now look down upon that tree. It is no longer just a hollow log, it is no longer just a tree, it is now a watercourse through which I will flow unto the barren land."

I looked, and I saw, and the desert became green, and the Earth that was parched and dry became green, not with rain that fell from Heaven, not because man had planted it, but because one tree had been broken, and now the desert began to blossom as a rose.

People of the Lord, thou hast said, "I will dedicate myself unto this ministry," but if thou art not willing to be that tree that is cut down, that tree that is hollowed out, I say unto thee that thou shalt never see the day when the nations and the barren places shall be filled with My glory. But if thou wouldst allow Me to do My work within thee, I promise thee that I shall carve My name upon thee. I will cause thee to be a byword among thy brethren. I will cause thy very heart to bleed until I am satisfied with that which I have done in thee.

The day will come when I will take many of thee from among thy brethren. I will cut thee off, and I will send thee to the nations of the Earth, and thou shalt dance over the nations, and thou shalt sing in the nations, and thou shalt move among the nations, and one shall put ten thousand to flight, and the water of God shall spring up, and the glory of the Lord shall cover the Earth as the waters cover the sea.

And I will restore to you the years that the locust hath eaten, the cankerworm, and the caterpillar, and the palmerworm, my great army which I sent among you. Joel 2:25

Chapter Three

The Parable of
The Wasted Years

TWO MEN CAME BEFORE THE King one day. Weary, and having travelled over many miles of desert, they came before Him. One was a young man who stood straight and tall, and the other was bent with the burden of many years. Now hear ye the parable of these men, and hear it well.

As they came into the courtyard, each bore in his hand a vessel. Approaching the King, both men knelt in His presence to give unto Him his vessel.

The young man said thus unto his King: "O King,

I give unto Thee everything that is in my vessel. Contained in this vessel are my hopes, my dreams, my strength, the force of my years, my plans and my desires. I give them unto Thee. If Thou wilt take this that I give unto Thee, O King, I shall give it to Thee, and it shall be Thine."

The King said, "I will take it."

The young man stood back as the older man came before the King. This man bowed low, and he said, "O King, I give Thee what is left in my vessel. I would give Thee the strength of my years and the force of my youth, but alas, it has been wasted, and it is not in my vessel to give unto Thee. I would give unto Thee my plans and my dreams, but they are not in my vessel. I can only give Thee what is left of a life. If Thou wilt take that which is left, I will give it unto Thee. I would give unto Thee all of the tears, and all of the heartaches, and all of the sorrows, and all of the experiences that life has brought unto me. I would put them in my vessel and give them unto Thee."

The King said, "I will receive them at thy hand."

The two men went away out of the presence of the King. The young man went his way, knowing that he had given to the King a full vessel, the older man knowing that he had given to the King only what was left of a life.

On another day there came a decree from the same King to these men. They appeared in the presence of the King and, sitting before the King, were their two vessels.

The King began to speak unto the younger man, and He said, "I will now take thy vessel, and I will pour it out." As He placed His hand upon the vessel to pour it out, the young man rose up to the King, and he said, "O King, hear Thou me. I gave Thee my life that Thou mightest use it, and that Thou mightest have it, but I would ask of Thee, pour it not out in this way and in this place. If Thou shalt pour it out thus, it shall be wasted. O King, if Thou wouldst only take it and let it be used in the manner I shall suggest, it shall surely become a great blessing unto Thy Kingdom."

The King said, "I hear thy words."

The old man stood, and the King said, "I would pour out thy vessel."

The older man began to cry, and he said, with tears streaming down his face, "Whithersoever Thou canst pour it out, O King, let it be poured out."

The King took him by the hand, and He led him to a wasted wilderness, a desert place. There He said unto him, "I would pour out what is left in thy vessel upon this dry ground."

Within the heart of the man there formed a question: "There is little left in my vessel, and what is it in this great wilderness? It is here that I have lived for lo these many years, and it was in this wilderness that I wasted my strength. It was in this wilderness that I lost my youth. It was in this wilderness that I shed my tears. Now the King doth say unto me, 'I would pour out what is left of thy life upon this dry ground.' If this is what He doth desire to do, I shall let Him do it, but lo, in my heart I cannot see that it will accomplish a thing."

The King said, "I will pour out thy vessel." Then He took it and poured it out upon the dry ground.

The King went his way; the older man went his way, and the years began to pass. On another day the King called again the two men before Him. He said, "I will take thee now and show thee what I have done."

To the young man He said, "Come, and I will show all of thy dreams and the force of thy youth. I will show thee thy ambitions and thy pleasures. Everything thou didst give Me, I will show it unto thee."

There, before them, on the golden table, they saw sitting their vessels, just as they were given unto the King – beautiful to look upon, the object of sacrifice. But the heart of the young man was sad, for he said, "It hath accomplished me nothing."

The King said, "Come with Me, and I will take thee to another place." He took the two men to the place which had been dry, and lo, a beautiful miracle had taken place. The dry ground had become an oasis. On every hand that which had been desert and that which had been of no account had sprung forth, and the Earth had become green for miles around. The Earth had become a splendor and a beauty and a glory. There were young people dancing upon the grass, and there were flocks and herds eating the grass. There was sun upon the land, and there was joy upon every hand. The King said unto the man, "Because thou didst give unto Me that which was left, and I poured it out upon the dry ground, it hath produced abundantly of life."

He said unto the young man, "It is not enough that thou give unto Me that which is thine. It is only enough if thou give it to Me and say, 'Thou shalt do whatsoever Thou wilt with that which I now give unto Thee.'"

Therefore, hear ye the parable and hear ye well: One man went away sad with his head hanging down, having given the King a full vessel, he went away sad. Another man, having given the King only half a vessel, stood and rejoiced. The latter end of this man was greater than the beginning because the Lord had done a miracle of pouring out upon him.

The Word of the Lord doth declare: "Better is the end of a thing than the beginning thereof." Hear ye, young men who be full of the strength of youth this day. Thou hast said over and over again, "I give Thee my life." Every time thou hast said it, I have reached out with My hand, and I have taken it. The young men and the young maidens in this place have given unto Me their vessels. But time after time there hath been within My heart a desire to pour it out, and they have said, "Yea, Lord, but if Thou will wait a minute I will tell Thee a better use for the thing which I have given Thee." They stand today in the House of the Lord, and though there is great joy in their heart, yet they know that their life hath not been poured out.

"There have been others who have wasted years in sin. There be others who have given unto Me only half a vessel, and there is condemnation upon them that does not come from My hand. They hang their heads down, and they say, 'If I could be but like the young men and the young maidens and give to the Lord all my life, then surely I could be among them rejoicing. Woe is me that I have only half a vessel to give unto my King.' "

Now hear ye the Word of the Lord: "If thou wilt give it unto Me and say, 'Pour it out wherever Thou wilt pour it out,' the Earth beneath thy feet shall become green. The Earth around thee shall become green, and that which was desert shall blossom as a rose," saith the Lord.

"Hear ye the parable of two men and hear it well. Therefore thou shalt again pour out thy life at My feet," saith the Lord.

Thou hast also given me the shield of thy salvation: and thy gentleness hath made me great.
2 Samuel 22:36

Chapter Four

The Parable of
The Secret of Greatness

*L*O, THESE MANY YEARS THERE hath been within my heart a deep cry that I might know the greatness of my God. When I was very young I counselled with myself, and I said, "I know that if I can but understand the greatness of my God, I will also then become great, for I have a desire to be great." I knew that it was born into the heart of every man that he might become great. I said, "I will search out books. I will get me learning. I will search. I will study, and I will get me learning, for by my much learning I will be great." I did this, but after I had searched and searched, I found that I was still not great!

I went among the sons of men with much knowledge in my heart and said, "I am not an eloquent man, therefore will I also search until I become eloquent." Therefore I did set myself to learn eloquence, until the day came when I could speak with great eloquence that which was within me, that which I had learned. I said, "Now will men acknowledge that I am a great man, for I can stand with eloquence and declare that which I have learned." This I did, but the sons of men turned sadly away, and I went again to my lonely place of sorrow saying, "I ache within myself, for I am still not a great man."

Then I said, "I know now what I need. I will be a man of power." Therefore I set myself to seek the face of my God, and I cried before Him, "O God, give me Thy power. Give me Thy power that I might heal the sick, that I might cleanse the leper, that I might assuage the pain of him who suffers."

Again I heard the voice of the Lord speak unto me, "If this is what thou dost desire, I will give it to thee."

I found myself able to lay my hands upon the sick and see them healed. I saw the leper cleansed, deaf ears being unstopped, and the latch string of men's tongues being loosed. As I marched among the sons of men, I said, "Now will men know that God hath made me great, for His power doth rest upon me, and I shall be great in the power of my God."

But though men followed me for the power which rested upon me, and though it was good to know that God did work with me, signs and miracles and wonders following, and though I knew that I could speak forth with eloquence that which I learned, yet the day came when I turned from the healing of the sick and ministering to those who were sad, and I turned from doing good, and I turned from meeting human need, and I said, "O God, Thou dost know and I know that I am still not a great man."

I then knew that if greatness would come to me, I must come and meet a great God. I found that everything I searched after did not make me great.

There came a day when I presented myself low before my God. I said, "God, if only Thou, in Thy great mercy, wilt but make me great."

I heard the voice of the Lord speak unto me, "Come with me, son of man, and I will now take thee to the Circle of the Earth. There on the Circle of the Earth, before the throne of thy God, bow low, and I will show thee the secret of greatness."

He took me up to the Circle of the Earth, beyond where the eagle flies, beyond where the wind blows, the moon shines or the sun doth ride in the heavens, there, where the throne of my God doth rest, He took me, and He said, "Now look down upon the sons of men."

And I saw a strange thing. I saw men strutting to and fro with books saying, "I am a great man." I saw men doing signs and wonders and saying, "I am a great man." And I saw men with great followings saying within themselves, "I am a great man."

I heard the voice of the Lord say unto me, "Son of man, now will I give thee Mine eyes, and thou shalt see greatness through them."

Then, a great miracle took place upon me, for as I looked again upon the Earth, I saw great men. The Lord said, "What seest thou, son of man?"

And I said, "O God, I see a wonder, I see a great wonder in the Earth. I see men who are great."

He said, "Look again, son of man." These were small men. These were very small men. They had no books, they had no power, they had no following, but I saw them stoop to bless a child. I saw them bend before the banner of His Name, and I said, "What is this? How can great men stoop low, for great men should stand before kings."

And the Lord spoke again unto me, and He said, "Look again, son of man." I saw great men bowed low in worship and, as they bowed in worship, and as they stooped to bless and pour out, I saw the

The Parable of The Secret of Greatness

hand of the Lord come and lift up small men and make them great.

Now hear ye the parable of the secret of greatness, ye who bear the Ark of the Lord. Hear the parable of the secret of greatness, ye who lead the people of God. Thy greatness is not in thine eloquence, nor in thine own importance, nor in thy power, nor is thy greatness in thy learning, nor yet is it in the fact that men come before thee and men follow after thee and men bow before thee. This is nothing more than the kings of the Earth have. The Lord hath spoken unto thee and said, "These are small men in mine eyes, but if thou wilt be great, thou shalt be low and bow in worship before thy God."

And know this, that if thou shalt bow low in worship before the Lord thy God, He will come unto thee, lift thee to the Circle of the Earth, and do a miracle within thy life, and thou shalt then face again the sons of men. It shall not be necessary unto thee that thou display learning, nor shall it be necessary unto thee that thou display power before the sons of men, nor shalt thou be driven to become one with authority over men, but thou shalt be one who has the ache in his heart satisfied, for thou hast bowed before a gentle God in worship, and His gentleness shall make thee great.

*He raiseth up the poor out of the dust, and
lifteth up the beggar from the dunghill, to set
them among princes, and to make them inherit
the throne of glory: for the pillars of the earth
are the Lord's, and he hath set the world upon
them.*   *1 Samuel 2:8*

Chapter Five

The Parable of
The Beggar In King's Clothes

I SAT ONE DAY AS A BEGGAR upon a dunghill. I sat, a poverty-stricken beggar. All that my ears could hear were the sounds of the dunghill on which I sat. All the sustenance I had was that given to me by compassionate men who saw my helpless plight. Dust blew in my face, and the heat of the sun beat upon my brow. I heard, but could not see. I heard the sounds of children playing, of dogs barking and the feet of those passing by me. I could not see the countenance of men, for I was blind and only knew the things of the dunghill upon which I sat.

Lo, as I was sitting upon my dust heap one day, there came a voice behind me saying, "I am He who does pick up the beggar and set him among princes." Then He touched mine eyes and, behold, a world was opened to me which I had never seen before! I was taken into a great house, and there He began to move upon me and work upon me. I did not see the countenance of Him who ministered unto me. All I knew at the time was that I had been brought into a large place. I had been taken from the dunghill and no longer felt the dust and no longer heard the voices of those who scrabbled in the streets. I had come into a large place. Then He took from me the garments of a beggar, clothed me with His own attire and set me at a table to eat food prepared for the King.

I rejoiced! One had lifted up a beggar, placed him in a large place, given him new garments and good food! As I drank freely of the wine and looked around, I saw other beggars, dealt with in the same manner, men who were also drinking freely of the King's wine.

When our hearts were merry with wine, we said one to another, "This is a good place." We laughed and sang, and we danced and rejoiced and looked at our garments. We said, "This is a good thing!

The Parable of The Beggar in King's Clothes

This is a good place! And this is good food!"

The servant came and spoke my name. He said, "Thou art wanted in the throne room." As I followed him, the joy of the wine no longer sufficed. The strength of the food was no longer sufficient. My garments seemed to me as inappropriate for one going before the King. As I entered the throne room, I bowed low and could not lift myself from the floor in the King's presence.

He said, "Dost thou know who brought thee from the dunghill?"

I said, "No."

He said, "One day, as I passed by, I saw thee in thy pitiful condition, and I said unto my servant, the chief servant of My household, 'Go, fetch that man and bring him to Me. Cleanse him from the dust of the way. Place upon him a kingly robe. Place upon him fresh garments. Feed him with royal food, and cause his heart to be merry with royal wine, and then bring him unto My presence.' "

Then the King said unto me, "Never again wilt thou go to the dung heap. Never again wilt thou be a beggar, for I will keep thee in My palace, and thou shalt wear My garments and eat My food. Thou shalt drink My wine and dwell among My servants."

My heart rejoiced at this good fortune, and I went

out from His presence with great gladness and rejoicing! What strange things were happening
to me!

Nevertheless I said to the King's servant, "Do not
ask me ever again to go into the presence of the
King. I am content to have my heart made merry
with His wine, to have my body strengthened with
His food, but I do not care to come again before His
awesome presence, for He has struck fear within
my heart. Surely, if I go in again, He will see that I
am but a beggar clothed in kingly garments."

But, the servant came to me yet again and
touched me and said, "Now, come, the King desires to see thee."

This time I said, "Nay, ask Him to see one of my
fellows, for surely I cannot go before the presence
of the King." Yet there was a drawing that came
from the throne room and I could not deny it.

As I came into the presence of the King, I bowed
low again. This time I was more loathe than ever to
lift up myself before Him, but He said, "Come.
What is this thing that I see? A heart that does not
long to come before the King? Art thou not grateful
for all that I have given thee, for all that I have done
for thee?"

From my heart these words escaped, "Yea, Lord,
but I am still only a beggar in king's garments."

The King said, "I know, and for this purpose

have I drawn thee unto Me. I will come now and touch thee, and thou wilt no longer be a beggar in king's garments. I will declare thee to be My son. I will never again call into My presence one who is a beggar in king's garments, but I will, from time to time, call into My presence My son."

As I knelt in His presence, I heard my voice begin to cry, "Abba, Father. Father, I am Thy son." I was no longer afraid of the King, for I was His son.

I went out from the King's presence, and those outside said, "What hath happened unto thee? Surely, some strange thing hath happened unto thee since thou hast gone before the King. Thou art no longer one of us." They ridiculed me, and they scoffed at me. They laughed at me and said, "Thou hast taken upon thyself too much, beggar, for with one word He can put thee back again upon the dunghill. We fear that King. We will serve Him all the days of our lives, for we desire not to go back to that dungheap. Thou takest to thyself too much, if thou are not afraid of that King!"

I was not able to bring to them the secret of the inner chamber: no father will cause his son to go back to the dunghill. Now, I stand in His presence and say, "Father, Father, Father, Father, Father, I am Thy son!" I worship Him ... and I worship Him ... I worship Him ... I worship Him ...

There is a path which no fowl knoweth, and which the vulture's eye hath not seen: The lion's whelps have not trodden it, nor the fierce lion passed by it. ... God understandeth the way thereof, and he knoweth the place thereof. Job 28:7-8 and 23

Chapter Six

The Parable of
The Solitary Man

AND NOW, UNTO HIM that hath an ear to hear, will I tell what the Lord hath done for me. There was a day when I walked among much people. We walked together to the House of the Lord, and there was much joy and much gladness among us, as we greeted one another and said, "Praise the Lord of Hosts, for the Lord is good, and His mercy endureth forever." We stood together in the House of the Lord, and we made sweet music together in the presence of our God. In that day I walked a wide road with much people.

I found among that people those with whom mine heart was knit and those from whose hearts I drew strength and fellowship, and I said, "Surely this is the good way." And I walked for many long years in this good way, and I said, "This is the way, walk ye in it." Many others joined and together we sang, and we rejoiced, and we danced, and we said, "Our God is so good."

But I tell thee, those who have an ear to hear, that I was not aware of the fact that the walls were narrowing upon the road we walked, and those who walked with me were becoming fewer and fewer. When I finally noticed it one day, I began to wonder within mine heart, "What is this strange thing that suddenly hath come upon me? I walk no more among a large group of people, nor do I walk among those who are constantly saying, 'Come with me to the House of God, for we will have fellowship together.'"

Even as I thus questioned, the road became narrower and the walls became higher, until I came to a place where, to my amazement, I stood alone, and the walls touched me on both sides. I stopped. Singing no longer rose from my heart. My feet were no longer joyful, dancing feet, and I said, "Something strange hath befallen me."

In that moment I heard a voice behind me saying,

The Parable of The Solitary Man

"This is the way, walk ye in it." I began to make my way through a very narrow place with room for only one to pass. I was alone. I heard the voices of those behind me singing, "Our God is a good God. Come thou with us, and we will do thee good." I heard the voices of those behind me, but I knew I was no longer among them, and the Spirit of the Lord came to me and said again, "This is the way, walk ye in it." And I walked the narrow road alone.

And in that hour, I was confronted with one whose image was like unto the Son of Man. My heart leaped within me, and I said, "The Lord has brought me to this place that I might meet Him. What shall I do? My song is no longer adequate, for I am in His presence. My dance is foolish. I dance the dance of a fool, for I am in His presence. I will put my hands up and praise Him."

But the walls were too narrow! And as I struggled, a voice behind me said, "Lift out thine hands and stretch them forth." And I found within my hands an alabaster box. I looked upon Him whose beauty was more than anything I have ever known. His countenance shone as the sun, even as the brightness of the Morning Star. He shone until my being was filled with light. And the walls gradually began to recede from me.

Within mine heart there were two cries. One cry

said, "Break the alabaster box, and do it now," but my flesh said, "See where this hath brought thee. Thou art standing alone. There is no man with thee. Thou art alone." As I wrestled with my flesh, the cry within mine heart and the light of the Morning Star shone so brightly within me that I took my alabaster box, and I broke it, and I poured it out upon Him. And it flowed and it flowed.

As the alabaster ointment began to flow, I fell on my face in worship before Him who had filled me with His presence. My flesh said, "I am alone," but my spirit cried out, "I care not that I am alone, for my eyes have seen the Morning Star." I worshipped, and I worshipped, and I worshipped, and I worshipped, and I worshipped. I worshipped, and I worshipped, and I worshipped, because mine eyes had seen the Morning Star, and I fell before Him as one dead.

Then in my spirit I said, "Surely I am a dead man. This must be Heaven, for I am in the heavenlies, and I have seen the Morning Star." And I worshipped, and I worshipped, and I worshipped, and I worshipped, and I worshipped, and I worshipped, for mine eyes had seen the Morning Star.

Then the Spirit of the Lord lifted me up and made me aware that I was no longer above, in the heavenlies, that I was indeed upon the Earth, and

The Parable of The Solitary Man

He made me aware that I was not alone, for I had thought that I heard only my own voice as I worshipped and worshipped and worshipped. The Spirit of the Lord spoke unto me and said, "Thou hast left a multitude to join a multitude, for these are they who worship the slain Lamb." They fell on their faces.

Now listen and thou shalt hear the sound of a great multitude of solitary men. And herein is a mystery that I cannot explain unto thee at this time: in the Kingdom of God there are those who cry, "Unity, unity, unity," and there is a group, the number of which is growing over the face of the Earth, and in the islands of the sea, and these be a group of solitary men who have been made one because they have seen the Morning Star. And they walk alone with Him; but they be one, and their voices are raised, "I worship, I worship, I worship." And together they sing the song of Moses and the song of the Lamb, and together they sing, "Hallelujah," for they are solitary men.

And I declare before Thee, O God, I care not this day where the former multitude hath gone nor where they shall go, for there are those whom Thou hast ordained that for them the wall will come closer and closer and closer, until the Morning Star shall shine upon them. And this is Thy doing, not mine, and I care not where they go, nor what shall occur among them. But my cry is, "O, let it never be that the light of the Morning Star shall be withdrawn from my soul, and let me always worship Him." I worship, I worship, I worship, I worship, I worship, I worship, I worship, I worship, I worship, I worship, I worship ...

And he said unto them, When ye pray, say, Our Father which art in heaven, Hallowed be thy name. Thy kingdom come. Thy will be done, as in heaven, so in earth. **Luke 11:2**

Chapter Seven

The Parable of
The Kingdom

THERE WAS BORN IN MY heart a cry, "Thy Kingdom come, O Lord!" And in the night season, and in times of great loneliness, a cry arose from deep within my soul, "O Lord, Thy Kingdom come. Thy Kingdom come."

In the zeal of my spirit, I cried unto the Lord and said, "O God, place me among those who are the tellers forth of Thy Kingdom. Surely, in this way, will I be part of the Kingdom of my God. If I can only be joined to those who have feet blessed upon the mountains and are beautiful."

The Lord did answer my cry. He joined me unto those who were the tellers forth among His people. For a season I went here, and I went there and busily told one after another, "Hear ye the Word of the Lord! Hear ye the Word of the Lord! Yea, the Kingdom of the Lord is at hand! Repent ye! Be ye converted! So shalt thou see the Kingdom of thy God!" For a season my heart was made glad, and I rejoiced among those who were the tellers forth of the Kingdom.

But a strange thing took hold upon me, and I found that I was not satisfied. I said, "O God, what is this strange thing that does come upon me? Surely to be part of the Kingdom I must be a teller forth." I looked around and saw men who were downcast, men who were in bondage and men who were in chains. I saw those who were sick and dying. I heard their moaning and groaning. I cried again unto the Lord and said, "O God, hear once more my cry and place me among those who be the healers, for I would be among those who, like the Son of God upon the Earth, did heal the sick and cleanse the leper and set at liberty those who were bound. I would be among those in whose hands is the power of God."

And the Lord did come unto me and set me

among the healers in His Kingdom, and within myself I said, "Surely now I will see the Kingdom of God established among men, for the blind are made to see, the deaf made to hear and the leper is cleansed. I see sickness leave. I hear the cry of joy from those who have been in bondage and are now delivered. I hear the demons cry as they depart from one whom they had held in bondage." I said within myself, "This doth bring me great joy, for I am among the deliverers, and this is the Kingdom of my God."

I went among the sons of men and said, "Behold, the Kingdom of God is come nigh unto thee." But even as the words escaped from my lips, something within me said, "Thou art still not satisfied." I went again unto the Lord, and I said, "O God, why am I not satisfied? Lord, there is still another cry within me. Place me among the scribes. O God, teach me of Thy Word."

And again the Lord came unto me and placed me among the scribes, and I found that which had been closed unto me was now opened by those who knew the Word of the Lord. I sat in amazement as the Word of the Lord did drop upon me. Then I ran with His Word and, in the haste of my spirit, I said, "This is the Kingdom of God, for surely the tellers forth do tell, the deliverers do deliver, and the scribes reveal the wonderful treasures of the Word of my God." But I was not satisfied.

I came again into the presence of my God and said, "O God, Thy Kingdom come. Thy Kingdom come. Place me among the prophets, for surely the trumpet shall sound in this last hour, and when the trumpet doth make a mighty sound, men shall listen and say, 'The Kingdom of God hath been established among men!' "

As I stood among the prophets I heard the Word of the Lord, and feverishly I ran here and there and declared, "Listen to the sound of the trumpet. Have thine ear opened wide, for 'Thus saith the Lord.' " I went here and I went there and said, "Thus saith the Lord. Hear the Word of the Lord."

But, sadly, I returned to the presence of my God and said, "O God, I have been among those who tell forth. I have been among those who deliver. I have been among those who study and shew Thy Word. Lord, in Thy mercy Thou hast even placed me among the prophets, and I have heard the sound of the trumpet. But I come to Thee now to say, 'Lord, I am not satisfied. I still am not satisfied.' "

The presence of the Lord came unto me. He took me to a gate by the wall and said, "Bow low."

And I said, "How low?"

And He said, "Lower yet. Lower yet. Lower. Lower."

When I came to a place in the wall, I saw a small gate, and as I stooped down, the Word of the Lord came to me. He said, "If thou wilt go through this gate, I will answer thy cry, for through this gate only worshipers enter."

I said, "But God, I have so much that I must take with me and the gate is so small."

The Word of the Lord came again unto me and said, "Only stripped men may go through this gate."

Sadly I laid aside everything. It was important to me that I be among those who ministered. But the Lord said, "I will have that, or thou canst not go through this gate."

Sadly I laid aside my ministry. I laid aside my trumpet. I laid aside my books and my learning and, sadly, yet with joy in my heart, I went through the small gate.

As I arose on the other side, behold, I found my trumpet! Behold, I found my books! Behold, I found my message! But it was no longer important to me, for the Lord had made me a worshiper. One who had been a teller forth, one who had been a deliverer, one who had been a scribe, one who had walked among the prophets had now been made a worshiper.

Now I stand before the presence of my God, and it is no longer important to me if the trumpet be in my hand or the message be in my tongue. It is only important that my God make of me a worshiper.

Now I put the trumpet to my mouth only when I hear the Father say, "Blow."

Now I can only speak when the Father says, "Speak."

It is enough now to bow low in His presence and worship Him.

Be patient therefore, brethren, unto the coming of the Lord. Behold, the husbandman waiteth for the precious fruit of the earth, and hath long patience for it, until he receive the early and latter rain. **James 5:7**

Chapter Eight

The Parable of
The Seasons

I HEARD THE VOICE OF THE Lord speak unto me, "Shepherd of My people, come up higher to the Circle of the Earth, for I have a word for My people." When I was lifted up, the voice of the Lord came unto me again, saying, "I will teach thee a parable of the seasons. Look thou now upon the Earth, and tell Me what thou dost see."

From the Circle of the Earth I looked, and I beheld the Earth. I saw that it was green, very green.

The Lord spake unto me, saying, "Draw near

unto the Earth." I drew near, and I saw that all living things were green. I saw that life was springing forth on the right hand and on the left. I heard the sound of the birds as they sang in the trees. I heard the sound of those who made merry in the springtime. I saw young men and young maidens dancing in the grass. I saw the leaves as they lifted their arms toward Heaven, and with garments of green, they danced before their God.

I heard the voice of the Lord speaking unto the wind as He released it from His fist, and He said, "Wind, go thou down and blow among the leaves. Go thou down and blow among the trees and the plants of the valley, and be thou upon the Earth as a pleasant wind."

Then I returned to the Lord and I said, "My God, I have seen it, and mine ear hath been opened wide, and I have heard the voice of springtime."

He said unto me, "Watch and see what I will do."

Then the voice of Him who commanded all things was issued upon the Earth. He said, "Sun, increase thine intensity upon the Earth. Wind, hold back from thy blowing. Rain, fall thou not upon the Earth, for it is time for change. Now, son of man, what dost thou see?"

I said, "I see those who were lovers in the springtime sitting now in great contentment, holding the fruit of their love in their arms. I see, in the heat of the day, plants bowing low. I see all mankind in the season of summer, and where the Earth is green in the spring, I now see the Earth blue and green and yellow and purple. I see roses, and I see all manner of flowers, and I smell the perfume that comes forth from the summer season."

The Lord spoke unto me and said, "Son of man, the Earth in the summer season is as a woman great with child, and being very, very great with child, she layeth aside the activity of the spring when the seed hath been deposited. She is heavy with child, and she groaneth to bring forth the fruit of her Earth. Now watch what I shall do."

He lifted me up, and He showed me as He spake again, and a season of change came upon the Earth. I beheld as He said, "Wind, thou art released to blow upon the Earth. Rain, thou canst now fall upon the Earth and, sun, release thine intensity. Now, son of man, return to the Earth and see what thou shalt see and hear what thou shalt hear."

He caused me to walk in the forest, and as I walked in the forest I looked, and I saw the beautiful color that was all around me. I reveled in the color of the new season which the Lord had brought upon the Earth. I said, "O, this is magnificent! This is beautiful!"

The word of the Lord said, "Let Me now open thine ear."

The Eye of the Needle

I heard the trees bemoaning themselves and saying, "Ah, alas, as much as we desire that it should not be, we, who once were green, are now beginning to show the signs of change. That wind doth blow! That sun is not as warm! That rain doth beat upon us! Though men look upon us and say we are beautiful, yet within ourselves we moan, for we know that the season of stripping is upon us! Woe, that wind shall strip us! It shall strip us until we stand bare and exposed by the will of our God."

The word of the Lord came unto me saying, "The Earth is a woman, great with child, and in the summer season she doth lay herself down to bring forth. As I cause the fall season to come, I cause strength to come upon her, and the fruit of the Earth is brought forth. Men gather the fruit of the Earth, even as one gathereth a newborn child and taketh it to himself. But she who hath brought forth that child layeth back upon the bosom of the Earth, and she doth rest, and she doth lay down, for she knoweth that her life hath brought forth upon the Earth. While men rejoice in the thing which the Earth hath brought forth, it is time for the Earth to rest."

"Now come with Me again and I will show thee another thing that I do." I stood before the Ancient of Days as He reached into His treasury, and He caused the snow to come forth. He said, "Snow, come thou forth from thy treasury and be thou put upon the Earth. Ice and wind and storm, be thou now upon the Earth."

I watched as the same Earth, which was green and beautiful and warm, became cold and frigid, as the whole Earth was stripped and laid bare, and the trees lifted bare arms before their God. The leaves of the trees fell to the ground, and creatures of the Earth hid themselves from the fury of the storm which did come upon the Earth. The Earth became deadly silent because the season of God's rest had come upon it. They which did bemoan themselves and say, "We be stripped," suddenly knew that it was the time for them to stand and receive again the rest of God.

As I returned to my God, He said, "Shepherd of this people, I have a word for this people from the parable of the seasons. Thou hast been through a springtime. Thou hast been through a summertime. There was a time when the maidens did dance, the young maidens and men did dance together in the presence of the Lord. They did play their instruments, and they did shout, and they did sing, and it was easy to make merry. The wind did gently blow, and the flute played, and the harp played, and the trumpet gave a certain sound, and men said one to another, 'It is a beautiful thing the

Lord doth do.' I who do decree the seasons say, 'It is spring upon that people.'

"As surely as I decreed the spring, I also decreed that the Earth, which was receiving the seed, should know the growth of that seed within it. In the summer season, thou didst become impregnated with seed, and truth did come unto thee, and thou didst find thyself heavy and ponderous with the truth of God. As much as the season of spring is not the season of bringing forth, nor yet is the summertime the season of bringing forth, so it hath been with this people.

"I decreed spring upon thee, and I decreed summer upon thee, and thou hast been large and impregnated with My truth. Thou didst cry, 'O, our God is stripping us. Our God is blowing upon us.' It was only for one reason, that that which was within thee should be brought forth and should be matured. It hath been brought forth, and that which has been brought forth is no longer thine, but it is Mine. I will cause it to grow and I will cause it to mature as the Spirit of the Lord doth be upon it.

"Thou art now moving into a winter season. Depending upon how thou dost take that winter season, thou shalt know a new impregnation of truth within thee. I will cause thee to rest and relax; even as she who has brought forth the precious

The Parable of The Seasons

fruit of the Earth doth relax and gather new strength, so am I gathering thee unto Myself that thou mightest have new strength. Thou canst not have spring, summer, fall and winter all in one season. That day will come, but it is not now. Thou art still creatures of time and, as creatures of time, I must work with thee by the seasons.

"Therefore, hear the parable of the seasons, and say not, 'Woe is us, for the Lord dealeth with us not today as He did yesterday,' but say, 'It is the season of the Lord that is upon us.' As surely as the season of the Lord is upon thee, the warm winds shall blow, and new truth shall spring forth again from the Earth."

Who hath ascended up into heaven, or descended? who hath gathered the wind in his fists? who hath bound the waters in a garment? who hath established all the ends of the earth? what is his name, and what is his son's name, if thou canst tell? Proverbs 30:4

Chapter Nine

The Parable of
The Wind

UPON A CERTAIN DAY THE voice of the Lord was issued from the Circle of the Earth. He who holdeth the wind in His fist gave command unto the wind, saying, "Go thou north wind and blow upon the Earth. South wind, go thou now and blow upon the Earth. East wind, west wind, from the fist of the Lord thou art released, to blow upon the Earth." At the command of the Lord, the winds went forth to blow.

It happened that the north wind blew upon the

waste places of the north, and he blew and he blew, and his blowing produced, through ice and snow, a strange and eerie sound as, at the command of the Lord, he blew upon the waste places of the north.

Searching vainly, the north wind went to find somewhere else to blow. Upon the tops of the mountains he blew; swooping down upon the north country, upon the mountains, he made a great noise. The creatures of the forest ran as the north wind came upon them, and the great sound did come as the north wind blew upon the mountains.

The south wind said, "I will blow. I will blow in the fair country. I will blow in the trees. I will blow among the ferns of the valley. The creatures of the field shall not run from me, for I will send forth a soft wind." Then there was a sound heard, which was made by the south wind. It was a fair sound. The creatures of the field stole out from their places of hiding, and the cool of the south wind blew upon them, and the trees of the field lifted their branches. The sound of going among the trees was heard as the south wind blew.

The east wind and the west wind consulted together, and they said, "We will go to the four corners of the Earth, and we will settle down upon the islands. With great fury we will whistle upon the islands, and the great sound of our fury will come as over land and sea we will go. We will cause the great, tall, splendid palm to bend by the force of our blowing."

The winds returned to stand before the presence of Him who gathered the wind in His fist, and they said one to another, "We must again return unto Him who did command us to blow."

"For though I blew," said the north wind, "among the waste places of the Earth, I produced only a lonely, howling, eerie sound, and it was not a certain sound."

The south wind said, "Though I blew softly upon the valley and upon the field, and although the trees did lift their branches, yet all I produced was the sound of rustling and going."

Sadly the east wind and the west wind met together in the presence of the Lord, and they said, "We, O God, consulted together, and we blew with great violence and great fury, and we blew upon the islands of the sea. We blew great waves upon the ocean. We caused the mighty palm to bow low before the fury of our blowing, but we produced no certain sound."

Then came the voice of the Lord and said, "Now, go again to the four corners of the Earth and blow once more upon the sons of men. This time thou shalt not blow upon the field, nor upon the ice field, nor shalt thou blow upon the islands of the sea, nor shalt thou blow upon the valley, but thou shalt blow upon My people. Strange and wonderful things shall occur as thou dost blow."

The winds did consult one with another and say, "We have never seen it on this wise before. The voice of the Lord doth command us to go and blow upon the people of God."

Therefore to do the bidding of the Lord, they came unto the people of God, and they began to blow. Lo, a strange thing happened, for the Lord did lift to the winds a pipe. The pipe had been hollowed out. The pipe was a reed which had been cut off from among its own. The pipe had had its life source taken away from it. The pipe had long since said, "I am but a dry stick. I have nothing. I have been hollowed out. My very heart has been taken out of me. There is nothing left of me. I am but a hollow instrument. I have holes in me. There is nothing left. The Lord Himself hath devastated me. I am ruined for everything except my God. I am no longer able to relate to my brethren as in former days. I am no longer able to do what I once did. I am only a dead pipe."

The Spirit of the Lord lifted that pipe, and then the voice of Him who gathereth the wind in His fist said, "Blow not upon that pipe, O winds, but blow *through* that pipe." As the wind blew through the pipe, the ear of the Lord was bent toward the sound that did come from the pipe which had been caused to be solitary; that pipe which had been cut off; that pipe which had been pierced. Lo, not the sound of great fury, nor the eerie sound of the wind as it howled in the north country, nor yet the fair sound of a wind that pleased the flesh of man, but a sound did arise unto the heart of God, a sound that did please His heart, the sound of a pipe – a certain sound!

As the wind of God did blow through the pipe, there arose a great cry from the midst of the people of God. "O God, cut me now off. Take me, prune me, pierce me here in my heart, for I too would be blown through by the wind of God."

As the winds returned again unto Him who had commanded them, the word of the Lord came unto them. "O winds of the Earth, thou hast blown over My people. Thou hast blown around My people. Thou hast blown upon My people. Thou hast blown upon the nations of the Earth at My command, but a new command hast thou heard from the voice of the Lord this day. There is a people who have been cut off, a people who have been hollowed out, a people who have been made ready to be blown through, that the voice of the Lord shall be heard in the land, and that the melody of Heaven shall begin to fall upon the ears of humanity. Therefore, wind of God, blow upon My people." Therefore the winds of God began to blow and blow and blow upon the people of the Lord.

I press toward the mark for the prize of the high calling of God in Christ Jesus.

Philippians 3:14

Chapter Ten

The Parable of
The High Places

THERE WAS A DAY WHEN A group of men stood together at the base of a great mountain, saying one to another, "We wonder what we would see, if we could climb to the height of that mountain. We wonder what we would see, if we could climb to where the eagle makes her nest." Taking counsel together, they said, "We will go, and we will conquer the mountain."

Lo, they laid upon the asses, the horses, and the men who followed them, much gear. It took them many days of planning and much gear and much packing, but there came a day when they went on their way toward the mountain, and they began to climb. As long as they climbed among the grasses and the trees there was shade for their heads, and there was soft grass under their feet. They sang a merry song, and they rejoiced, and they would stop and rest, drinking from the brook. And they said, "This is an easy thing we have set out to do."

As they ascended further, they found that rocks replaced the grass, and there were no trees. The elements began to beat upon them, and their progress became slower. There were among them those who became discouraged, and they said, "Go thou on. We will go back to a pleasant place where there is much water and many trees. We will stand by, and we will watch thee as thou dost ascend the mountain. Godspeed as thou dost travel the mountain." And they departed.

Those who went on encouraged themselves because they looked to the top of the mountain, and they saw the eagle in her nest, and they said, "We will ascend to that mountain to see what it is that the eagle doth see. There is a cry within our spirit that we might ascend until we be free, that we might go where the wind blows free, where the bird flies free, where the air is free, and where we be close to our God."

They ascended even higher, and they came to a

plateau. There they found a rough dwelling place, and they sat together and refreshed themselves and took shelter. They went through the things they had brought with them from the valley and counselled one with another saying, "This we must leave here. This was important to us when we left, but we cannot carry it any higher. We must leave some of our heavy possessions behind. We must lighten our load because the vision is becoming more clear."

When those men left that place where they had been resting, there was a great deal of debris left behind. All of it was valuable, but it could not be taken to a higher place. The men had carried too many possessions, but now these were left behind as the men continued to ascend.

The climbing grew worse. The wind beat upon them, the sun was hot, and at night the bitter cold closed in upon them. They said one to another, "We wonder if we should turn back and go to the valley below."

Something within them said, "Lift up thine eyes unto the hills from whence cometh thy help; thy help cometh from the Lord which made heaven and Earth."

They said, "We will go on."

Hear ye, ye people of the Lord. This is the thing they did. They sat together in the night season, and they made a commitment unto the vision which they held within their hearts. While some of their party stayed below in the pleasant place, these men set themselves to climb.

They toiled on until there were only two men left. They had no more possessions now. All they had was the vision that had been given to them as they stood at the base of the mountain. I wonder what the eagle sees when she sits in her nest, and I wonder what she feels when she stands on the highest mountain and surveys the world!

Totally committed to the vision, totally committed to the thing that was in their hearts, they again reinforced themselves by giving up everything that was a load unto them. These two men ascended the mountain until the climb seemed almost impossible. Yet they held not back, but continued to ascend until they neared the top.

As they drew near to the crest of the mountain, something took hold of them, and a great joy began to swell within them. They did not look back upon the men at the base of the mountain, nor to their possessions halfway up, but they said, "We are committed to the cause of His glory, and we will stand with the eagle on a high place." The joy that they received became a strength unto them.

There came a day when they climbed the last foot of the mountain, and a great joy came to them, for when they stood on that mountain they saw not just the green valley, they saw the world as the eagle sees it.

I would have thee to know, ye people of the Lord, that this is a parable which thou shalt learn, and thou shalt learn well. For there was a day when many among thee took a look at the mountain of God, and thou didst say, "Come, let us go up to the mountain of the Lord." Thou didst take with thee thy possessions, and thou didst take with thee thy relationships, and thou didst take with thee many things that were good and right and proper, and many of thee were laden down. The Lord smiled upon thee, and His grass was green under thy feet, and the sun was warm upon thee, and the trees sheltered thee.

There came a day when the Lord allowed thee to rest in a middle place, and He said, "There, this is the place where thou shalt go through thy things and leave behind that which is not necessary for the journey, and this is the place where thou shalt recommit thyself to the vision, and this is the place where thou shalt recommit thyself unto that which thou shalt take into My Glory."

There came a day when some moved aside and said, "We cannot pay the price." This is the word of the Lord unto thee: "I am the God of all living things, and I open My hand, and I satisfy the desire of every living thing. If that is as far as thou dost desire to go, then thou shalt find much possessions that have been left behind, and thou couldst have a good life there. But, if there are those in whom the vision of thy God burns until it almost consumes thee, then know this, that thou art approaching a time of commitment – not to one another, not to the work of God, but to the glory of the Lord. Thou shalt stand in the presence of thy God, and thou shalt say, 'O my God, I am committed to Thy glory. I will desire only Thy glory, for Thou hast put it within my heart to go high and fly where the eagle flies and see what the eagle sees and be renewed like the eagle is renewed.' "

God thundereth marvellously with his voice; great things doeth he, which we cannot comprehend. For he saith to the snow, Be thou on the earth; likewise to the small rain, and to the great rain of his strength. Job 37:5-6

Chapter Eleven

The Parable of
The Snow

THERE WAS A DAY WHEN I stood in the midst of the people of God, and the hand of the Lord fell heavy upon me. The word of the Lord came unto me, saying, "Come now with Me, for I have indeed something to say unto thee."

He lifted me to the Circle of the Earth, and I stood beside Him in whose sight the nations are but a drop in the bucket. I stood beside Him whose feet rested upon the footstool of the Earth. I stood beside the Ancient of Days who holdeth the wind in His fist.

The word of the Lord came unto me, "I have somewhat to say unto thee concerning the parable of the snow. What seest thou, son of man?"

I looked upon the Earth, and I saw men dwelling carelessly. I said, "Lord, I see men dwelling carelessly."

He said, "Look again. What dost thou see upon the hillsides?"

I answered, "Lord, I see the beasts of the field dwelling in peace, and I see the animals of the forest in security, fat and flourishing."

He who holdeth the wind in His fist said, "Look now, son of man, what I do," and He released the wind. He said, "O thou wind, go thou now and blow upon that mountain. Thou shalt not blow in fury upon the mountain, but thou shalt blow upon that mountain."

In obedience to the word of the Ancient of Days, the wind gathered itself and blew upon the field, and it blew upon the trees, and it blew upon careless men, and it blew upon contented beasts. Even the trees swayed.

The Lord opened mine ear, and I heard the leaves talk one to another. They said, "We be blown upon by the wind of God. It is the season of change."

The beast of the field said one to another, "It is no longer time for us to lay in contentment, for with the blowing of the wind there cometh a change."

The Parable of The Snow

Therefore the beasts of the field, at the bidding of the wind, found themselves holes. They found themselves clefts in the rocks. The small animals digged into the Earth, and the leaves began to lift a glory that they had not known; for there had been a wind that had blown – the wind of change.

The Ancient of Days spoke again to me. He said, "Watch now what I do." He called back that wind, and it came into the fist of the Ancient of Days. He said, "Now, stormy wind, thou stormy wind that doth fulfill My will, I now command thee, Go thou and blow upon that mountain."

The stormy wind of God began to blow upon that mountain, and it whistled through the valley, and it marched up the mountain slope, and it arose as it tore from place to place across that mountain. A strange thing did happen as the wind began to blow: the snow came.

The word of the Lord came unto me, "From this snow I will teach thee a parable, son of man. Give this parable unto the people of God. For even as the wind of God hath blown and change hath come, so hath the furious wind of My Spirit blown. It hath blown and blown until snow hath begun to fall, and the snow of Lebanon hath begun to fall.

"Men have said, 'Our God is angry with us, for the wind of God doth blow in fury.' It is not so."

As He carried me again to the Circle of the Earth, He bade me to look. I saw that everything was covered with snow and all of nature bowed its head before Him who had caused the snow to come.

Then again the Ancient of Days spoke and He said, "Once again would I send the wind. This time, stormy wind, remain in thy place. This time, chilly wind, remain in thy place, but, warm wind, blow." Across that mountain a warm wind began to blow, and there was an awakening from deep within the Earth, and underneath the snow there was activity. The beasts of the field were stirred within themselves. The animals of the forest shook the snow from themselves, and they said, "It is a warm wind that doth blow. The season of change is again upon us."

From underneath that snow, water began to pour. Down the mountain side, as the word of the Lord came to me, He showed me the waterfall as it fell down the side of the mountain. He showed me the brook as it went babbling across the meadow. Again and again and again, the warm wind blew until more water and more water and more water came. Every time the wind blew, the water became more and more furious and more violent as it cascaded down the side of the mountain.

The word of the Lord came again to me, "Now, would I teach thee this thing that I am saying unto thee. For every time the snow doth come, there shall also follow it a warm wind that will cause the water to fall. When the water doth fall, it shall flow in individual rivers. But there doth come a time when one river doth meet another, and the other river doth meet another river. Together they form a procession. The waters of the mountain become a procession toward the sea. All of nature doth stand back as the waters of God march to the sea. My people have been individual brooks and rivers and waterfalls. They have resisted the cold wind of change."

The word of the Lord would come unto this people, "Thou shalt not be the same from this day, for He who sitteth upon the Circle of the Earth did cause a wind to blow upon thee, and thou didst say, 'There is change coming. We feel wind. Something is happening. There's wind.' It did herald the change. It did herald a new season."

Hear ye, and hear ye well. The word of the Lord from the heart of thy God, this day, shall come unto thee from the parable of the snow.

"I caused also a cold wind to blow upon this people. It blew furiously, yea, it blew furiously, and there were those who hid from the blowing of the wind because it brought the cold snow.

"I have also, this day, released a warm wind that doth cause the snow and the ice to melt, and the streams and rivers to flow into the ocean. There will come a day when, if thou will let the wind of God blow upon thee, that I will cause thee to become one in a way that thou hast never known. Thou shalt no longer be the waterfall that falleth from the mountain. Thou shalt no longer be the brook that floweth by itself across the meadow; but thou shalt be one with the mighty river of God that is formed in this last hour that shall march in procession toward the sea. Thou shalt know the day when the abundance of the sea shall be converted unto thy God, and therefore shalt thou lift thy hands and worship."

Therefore shalt thou know that this day the Ancient of Days hath indeed lifted His hand, and from His fist He hath caused another wind to begin to blow. Ye people of the Lord, the wind of change is blowing, and thou shalt not resist the wind of change, but thou shalt lift thy banners and join with the people of God. Lift thy banners in thy procession toward the sea, and the abundance of the sea shall be converted unto Him.

Thou wilt keep him in perfect peace, whose mind is stayed on thee: because he trusteth in thee. Isaiah 26:3

For he is our peace, who hath made both one, and hath broken down the middle wall of partition between us; Ephesians 2:14

Chapter Twelve

The Parable of The Way of Peace

OR LO THESE MANY YEARS, there hath been a thing which caused my heart to be torn within me. It is the bondage of the people of God. For there was a day when the Lord did speak unto my spirit and say, "I have called thee to be a shepherd." And from the hour when the Lord placed within me the shepherd's heart, the cry of my heart hath been, "O God, give me sheep that are truly free, give me sheep that are liberated." The desire of mine heart hath been that upon the hill-sides of Zion the sheep might play, in the sunshine the sheep might laugh and dance, being protected by the oil and by the crook and by the presence of the Shepherd.

There came a day when that which was within me overwhelmed me and I said, "I shall go to war." It is not my desire, nor is it the desire of the Lord, to have sheep who merely graze on the pasture and go from one place to another but are not free. Therefore I said, "I will put aside the implements of a shepherd, and I will take unto myself the instruments of a warrior."

Within me the heart of a warrior did begin to stir. I placed upon mine head the helmet of salvation. I shod myself with the preparation of the Gospel of peace. I had within mine hand the sword of the Spirit and the shield of faith, and I knew that I was well equipped to go to war.

When I decided that I would become a warrior, there were those around me who said, "If thou shalt go to war, we shall go with thee." So, together we became warriors in the Kingdom of our God, deciding that the sheep must be set free. And surely as we went to war against the workings of the enemy there was great bloodshed. The enemy was smitten on the right hand and on the left, and we said one to another, as we encouraged ourselves in the thing which we were doing, "A thousand shall fall at our side, and ten thousand at our right hand, but it shall not come nigh us."

As we went from one place to another, making war, we said one to another, "Our God is a God of war. We be warriors. Onward! Onward ye warriors."

There was great victory. We saw people in chains, and those chains were broken. We saw high towers come down, and together we rejoiced, and we said, "Ah, we be warriors in the Kingdom of our God. The towers come down, the chains fall off. There is liberty here. There is joy here." As we went forth to war, we comforted ourselves because our spirits rejoiced in the Lord.

But there came a time when the word of the Lord came a second time unto me: "The God of peace shall bruise Satan under thy feet shortly."

I said, "But God, see my battle scars; see those who have been released; see the enemies who have been slain; see the high towers that have come down."

And the word of the Lord continued to come: "The God of peace shall bruise Satan under thy feet shortly."

I said to those who made war with me, "A strange thing has occurred. There is within my spirit no desire to go forth to battle."

There were those who said, "Thou hast not heard the word of the Lord, for surely it is the desire of our God that every man should be set free." I knew that the thing they said was right. It *is* the desire of the Lord that every man should be set free. But as I sought His face, I heard the word of the Lord: "The God of peace shall bruise Satan under thy feet shortly."

And I began to cry, "No longer do I ask of Thee, O God, sharpen my sword; make me skillful with the shield; no longer put a steed under me that will go quickly into the warfare, but O God, give me the instrument of peace."

Then the word of the Lord came again unto me, saying, "Take up thy crook, take up thy horn of oil, place upon thee the Shepherd's coat, and I will add this to thee: thy sheep shall graze in peace because I shall put peace *within* thy spirit. Thou shalt not go against the enemy with a spirit of turmoil, but thou shalt go against the enemy of the flock with a spirit of peace, for I *am* thy peace."

And the Lord has done a beautiful thing within my spirit. He is Lord! There is no need to go to war. He is Lord! There will be times when theWord of the Lord will come again, and He will say, "It is time to go to war. But at that time thou shalt place upon thyself the armor which I give thee, and thou shalt go to war, but there shalt be no war within thine own spirit. It shall not be thy sword that will thrust the enemy through; it shall not be thy shield that shall frighten him, but it shall be thy total peace. It shall be thy total peace that shall cause the enemy to flee from thy borders. Thy God is thy peace, ye people of the Lord; He is thy peace, for He is Lord!

Tell me, O thou whom my soul loveth, where thou feedest, where thou makest thy flock to rest at noon: for why should I be as one that turneth aside by the flocks of thy companions? If thou know not, O thou fairest among women, go thy way forth by the footsteps of the flock, and feed thy kids beside the shepherds' tents. Song of Songs 1:78

Chapter Thirteen

The Parable of The Worshiping Shepherd

LO, FOR THESE MANY YEARS have I been a shepherd. The delight of my life hath been to lead the people of God. Morning by morning I arose with but one desire in my heart, and that was to lead the people of God where the Great Shepherd did lead. Morning by morning I arose with great joy because again I knew the Shepherd of Israel would lead the flock of His pasture.

There were times when the flock did go into dangerous areas, and the Shepherd of Israel would say,

"O, be thou a faithful shepherd, and bring them back from the place of falling, and the place of danger, to the place of security."

There were times when I did join myself to the other shepherds by the watering hole, and the sheep did freely mingle back and forth, as I fellowshipped with the other shepherds. It was at such times that the Great Shepherd of the sheep would come among us, and we were glad that we could say, "Unto this calling have we been born, that we be shepherds."

It was among the sheep that I learned to dance. It was among the sheep that I learned to play skillfully upon my instrument. It was among the sheep, when they rested at noontime, that I learned to sing unto my God and to make sweet melody. It was among the sheep that I learned the weapons of my warfare, for when the lion and the bear came against the sheep, even the Shepherd of Israel gave me power, and I smote the lion and tore apart the bear. The Lord taught me that there were weapons of warfare which are given unto a shepherd.

I did at night rest my flocks by the shepherds' tents. There were times, in the dark of the night, when my heart would awaken me, and strange things would take hold upon me. In the daylight hours these things left, and again I would leap and skip and dance and rejoice with the sheep.

The Parable of The Worshiping Shepherd

I would inspect one sheep and then another, and it was the delight of my life to pour oil upon the head of each sheep that he might not be bitten by the adder as he went into the pasture that day. It was the greatest joy of my life to see fat sheep and much wool.

But in the night season, when the sheep were bedded down and the other shepherds were sound asleep, my heart stirred within me, and I could not understand the strange and empty feeling which took hold upon me. I would arise in the night season and walk beneath the stars and would say, "Surely, this is a strange thing that has come unto me. I have always been a shepherd. The Lord has called me to this, and I love to shepherd the flock. Why then am I empty and dissatisfied in the night season?"

In the morning when I arose, the feeling would not leave me, and suddenly I knew that I was "sick of love." I knew that no longer could I be content to feed the sheep, to lead them to good pasture, to dance among the sheep, to play among the sheep, to laugh with the sheep, to pick up the wounded among them. No longer could I be satisfied to deliver them and to see them in safety in the camp. My heart had stirred within me in love for the Great Shepherd of Israel.

I said nothing of the thing that was within my

heart. The other shepherds would have ridiculed me and cast me out from among them saying, "Thou shalt not be among us." Therefore, my heart was disquieted within me – until a day when there appeared in the desert the Shepherd of Israel. He took me by the hand, and He said, "Come with Me."

My heart answered, "Draw me, and we will run after Thee."

And as He took me over the desert, I was not aware of the place to which He brought me until mine eyes were opened, and I saw the gates of the palace. Then I said, "O, I am black, but I am comely, as the tents of Kedar, and as the curtains of Solomon. The sun hath kissed me, and I am dark." But He took me in.

I looked back upon the sheep, and my heart was torn for the sheep. I thought they would be scattered upon the mountains of Israel, and the lion and the bear would then get them. But the Shepherd of Israel said, "Mind not the sheep, but come after Me."

He took me into His banqueting house and said, "Lift up thine eyes." I saw that His banner over me was LOVE. I sat down under His shadow with great delight, and His fruit was sweet to my taste. Contented, I sat under the shadow of the Shepherd of Israel until again I heard His voice. He said,

The Parable of The Worshiping Shepherd

"Rise up, my love, and come away, for the time of the singing of birds is come. The rain is over and past. The flowers appear on the Earth. The voice of the turtle is heard in our land. The fig tree putteth forth her fruit. The season of love is upon us."

I said, "I cannot come, for I am not clothed to live in the palace of the King. Surely Thou hast only brought me here to visit. Surely Thou hast only brought me here to feed me and give me good things that I might again go back to tend the sheep."

He said, "Nay, I would put thee into the custody of the keeper, and He shall clothe thee with garments that thou hast never dreamed of."

I was loathe to give up my shepherd's cloak. I said, "No! Put those garments upon me, but I will not let my cloak go!" But for the disquietment of my heart and for love of the Great Shepherd of Israel I said, "Take my cloak. Take my crook. Take my horn of oil. I will be clothed to go in unto the King."

Lo, there I found garments more glorious than anything I dreamed could have come to one born to be a shepherd.

Then the keeper said, "Come now with me." He took me, not into the outer chamber, nor yet into the banqueting hall, nor yet into the throne room. He took me into the very presence of the King, He who has appeared unto me as the Great Shepherd, He whom I had so admired as the Great Shepherd, had come unto me now as my King. I fell before Him in adoration and in worship. He who had won me in love as the Great Shepherd had now come to reveal Himself to me as my King.

When I arose from His presence, my heart was stirred within me toward the sheep, but the King said, "Come with Me." We went together into the pasture, and there were my sheep. They were no longer truly mine, for when I had surrendered my cloak to the King, the sheep became His sheep. They were fat. They were flourishing. They were covered with wool. They were frolicking. They were leaping. They were rejoicing. There was no bear. There was no adder, for they fed in the King's pasture, and they had become part of His flock.

Now gladly do I lay aside my shepherd's cloak that I might become one with the King. Gladly do I take the sheep which had been mine and give them unto Him, that they might become His. Their wool shall be His. Their fatness shall be His. Their goodness shall be added to the wealth of His Kingdom, while I delight myself in the King.

Now I dance no more for joy of the sheep. It was there I learned to dance, but now I dance to please the King. Now I no more sing my song to quiet the sheep, for the sheep have no need of quieting. They

The Parable of The Worshiping Shepherd

are in the pastures of the King. I sing now out of adoration for my King. I play skillfully upon my instruments, not to pass away idle hours, nor to cause the other shepherds to rejoice, for I know not where the other shepherds have gone, and I care not where they be. I care only that my skillful playing on my instrument should bring gladness to the heart of my King.

The LORD is nigh unto them that are of a broken heart; and saveth such as be of a contrite spirit.   Psalms 34:18

The sacrifices of God are a broken spirit: a broken and a contrite heart, O God, thou wilt not despise.   Psalms 51:17

Chapter Fourteen

*The Parable of
The Broken Heart*

I WILL TEACH THEE THE PARable of the broken heart.

As I moved among the sons of men, I experienced rejection from my brethren, and I wept many tears, and I lay before the Lord and said, "God, surely this rejection hath broken my heart. I will come before Thee now with a broken heart."

I presented before my God, in the high place, a heart that was broken. He gave it back to me, and sadly He said, "Son of man, return unto thy place, for this heart which thou hast given me is not broken. It is bruised, but it is not broken."

I went again among the sons of men and pursued my activities. Relationships began to fall from me, and those whom I loved began to turn their backs upon me, and I wept again copious tears, and I said, "Surely this time I am one with a broken heart. I will present unto my God a broken heart."

I ascended into the high place, and I gave unto my God my broken heart. He looked at me with compassion, and He said, "Son of man, thine heart is bruised, but it is not broken; therefore I return it to thee now. Go again among the sons of men."

"This time," I said, "I will not worry about a broken heart, but I will go among the sons of men, and I will sing my songs to bless the Body of Christ. I will minister the Word of the Lord with joy, victory, and gladness."

In the secret place I knelt before the Lord and I said, "God, I am a total failure;, I sing my songs, I play my instrument, I speak Thy Word, but I am a failure. Surely this time, Thou hast broken my heart. If indeed Thou hast said I am nigh unto them that be of a broken heart, I draw nigh unto Thy presence, oh my God, to give to Thee a heart that is broken. If my heart was not broken by rejection, if my heart was not broken by relationships, then surely, this day, as I present to Thee a heart that has

The Parable of The Broken Heart

been broken by failure and lack of success and rejection from all sides, this time I give to Thee my broken heart."

As I bowed low before the throne, sadly He said, "Son of man, thou hast not yet learned the parable of the broken heart. This time go not among the sons of men and pursue thine activities."

He arose and took me by the hand to a place called Calvary, and there, as I knelt in His presence, I saw His love, and suddenly I felt the heart within me begin to break. I heard Him say, "I will take away the heart of stone, and I will give thee a heart of flesh. I will give to thee a broken heart."

As I knelt before Calvary, my heart broke within me, not this time by my failures, by my rejection, by my broken relationships, but my heart was broken by His love. As the love of my God enveloped me, I looked down upon my failures, and they were but nothing. I looked upon my broken relationships, and I said, "They be but nothing in the light and the love of my God."

When I arose from that place, I ascended again into the high place of my God. I reached to give to Him my broken heart, because this time I knew my heart had been broken by His love. When I presented it to Him, He reached out and received from me my broken heart, and when He returned my heart, it was no longer broken and useless in my hand, but it was filled with love.

Though my life lay at my feet in ashes, though my hopes and my dreams were in ashes at my feet, though my relationships were broken and my life seemed like a failure, yet I moved. I moved among the sons of men, pouring love from my heart. Suddenly, I realized I was no longer a failure because my God hath drawn nigh unto me through my broken heart.

The word of the Lord unto this people is: "Yes, I called thee to war. Yes, I have called thee to be warriors, but thou art ineffective, and thou shalt not do the work of the Lord until thou hast come before the Lord with a heart that has been broken by My love. I have not called thee to hate thine enemy; I have called thee to love thine enemy. I have called thee to minister through peace. I will come to thee as a new dimension of My love and a new dimension of My peace. Therefore, no longer cry over thy failures and thy broken relationships, nor cry over those things of yesterday that now lay at thy feet in ashes, but arise and worship thy God in a new dimension; for I am the God who draws near to men of a broken heart."

Ask of me, and I shall give thee the heathen for thine inheritance, and the uttermost parts of the earth for thy possession.   Psalms 2:8

Chapter Fifteen

The Parable of
The High Road

When I was very young, and my years weighed light upon me, there was a day when the Spirit of the Lord came unto me, and He filled me with His Presence. In that hour men said unto me, "Young person, thou art mad, for thou art not like other ones. Thou dost not do what other men do." But there was a thing that was planted deep within my soul for I had tasted of something that is called "the Presence of my God."

But as the years piled upon me, life for me became heavy and complicated, and as I walked with my God I heard many voices, and they said unto me, "Come with us, and we will do thee good. Come with us, and walk with us. It is not necessary that thou walk alone. Thou hast said unto us that thou dost walk alone with thy God, and this is a thing that we understand not, for we too have met our God."

I went with them, I laughed with them and talked with them, and I did what they did. I went where they went, and I saw what they saw. As I went among them, my heart was made glad and, for a season, I rejoiced, and I said, "I can have the presence of my God and still walk with these who walk on the lower level."

But there came a voice in the dead of the night saying unto me, "Unto every man cometh a high way and a low, and in between on the misty flats the rest drift to and fro. Son of man, thou shalt decide which way thy soul shalt go."

In that hour I fell before my God, and I said, "If Thou wilt only come unto me and fill me with Thy Presence, I will no longer walk in the middle. I will no longer walk on the lower path, nor will I walk with those who drift to and fro. I will not walk with those who are tossed about with every wind of doctrine; I will not ever again concern myself with the things that consume the hearts of normal men."

The Parable of The High Road

In that hour He said unto me, "Come with me, and I will take thee to the Circle of the Earth, and in the Circle of the Earth I will show thee a thing among my people."

And as quickly as He spoke unto me He took me up to the throne of His Presence, and there He let me look upon the people of God that are called "the Body of Christ." He showed me people marching and busy, and He said unto me, "Son of man, look with My eyes, not with thine."

I saw there were those who cared only that the day would come when they had made their peace with God, and they knew that this was all that they required.

Then He said, "Now, go among those who are busy with the things of time, and I will talk unto thee concerning these things."

He dropped me into the midst of a people, and He said, "Listen to what they say."

As I listened to them, my heart was made sad, for I heard them talking of finances, and I heard them talking of clothing, houses and lands, and I heard them talking of all the things that they were busy with. He said, "Now, come up again, and I will show thee what is happening."

He showed me, on a high level, that the enemy of their soul had gone ahead of them on the pathway, and into one heart he threw a house and into another heart he threw apples, into another heart he threw gold, and into another heart he threw wrong relationships. As they marched down the highway, they began to pick these things up, and as they picked them up, they became diversions. The Spirit of the Lord then said unto me, "This is what the enemy has done unto My people. They have looked to the right, to the left, and been diverted from My presence."

He said, "Now come again with Me, and I will show thee a strange thing. I will take thee to a solitary people, and I will take thee to a people who have had a meeting with Me at the burning bush."

And lo, I saw a people marching upon a high road, marching upon a path that no fowl knoweth, the birds of the air have not discovered it, neither have the beast of the field walked thereon, but there was a path that had been laid, and it was laid from Earth to Heaven, as even Jacob's ladder was laid. And He said, "I have snatched from among this group a people, and I have set them upon this pathway."

From time to time He caused me to look at those who were busy with things, other things and not His presence began to taunt them. But there was a solitary spirit about them, and they said, "We care not what thou doest, nor do we care how thou livest, nor do we care what thou sayest, for there was a day when we met our God, and He filled us with His presence."

As they walked before their God, a strange thing happened unto them. From time to time solitary men would fall on the pathway. No man sought to pick them up; no man sought to cause them to walk. They merely walked around them for they said again, "They have met their God. They have fallen before their God."

The Lord said, "Now will I lift thee up, and I will take thee out of time, and I will show thee into the realms of tomorrow, and what shall happen."

I saw a wall of fire, and I said, "O God, I thought I would like to be among that solitary people, but I will not walk through fire again. I have walked through fire so much, I will not walk through it again."

He said this unto me, "Thou hast only met fire; thou hast not walked through fire, but I will take this people and watch what I do."

As the Spirit of the Lord came down, He took them through the fire. I said, "God, they will be destroyed."

He said, "No, oh thou of little faith, Daniel was not destroyed. Shadrach, Meshach and Abednego were not destroyed, but rather they came out of the fire, and only that which had clothed them was

119

burned. I tell thee that as I take thee through the fire I do a new thing in thee."

I said, "Let me join them, let me join them, let me join them."

He said, "This time we walk together through the fire," and He took my hand, and He walked me and others through the fire. But I knew not that there were others, for He had made of me a solitary man.

I said, "I care not where they go, I care not what they do, I want only the presence of my God."

Again He said, "Now come."

He took me again to the Circle of the Earth, and there on the Circle of the Earth, held in the hand of Him who holds the wind in His fist, He said, "Look," and I saw those who had walked through the fire had BECOME fire, and fire had consumed them. They had not MET a burning bush, they had BECOME one. I heard the word of the Lord speak these words unto me: "Son of man, return thou unto My people and tell them this, 'It is a new day. This is the dawn of a new day. I am bringing men to choose whether they want the low road or the high road or they want to drift in the middle. Only solitary men will walk with Me into the new day. They will become a burning bush in the Earth, and it will not be that I need to send an army to the nations. I will send a MAN to the nations; I will send a man who has BECOME my burning bush. And look what I do."

He picked one after another up, and He put them into a nation, and I watched as He put one in the island of Taiwan, and suddenly Taiwan began to blaze with the fire of God. He said, "See, one with Me is a majority."

I saw where the curtain of China closed, and I stood on the outside, and I wept much about it, and I said, "God, but Thou has promised us China."

He said, "Thou of little faith, watch what I do."

He picked up a handful of men, and He dropped them, and they set the land of China ablaze.

He said, "Come with me to India." As He showed me India, and He said, "I am doing a new thing in India. I am taking now a people who have BECOME the fire of God, and I am scattering them among the millions of India, and as I put fire in India, India will burn for My glory."

Now hear, people of the Lord, this is the word of the Lord unto this people: thou art in a time of choice. Thou wilt choose a low road, thou wilt choose a middle road, or thou wilt choose My presence.

The word of the Lord would come unto thee this day: "If thou choosest My Presence, I will strip you until there is nothing left but My glory. I will take from thee the petty little things thou dost think are needed, and I will take from thee everything that thou dost value except My presence, and My presence shall come and consume thee, and thou shalt walk with Me into a new day.

"There are among this people those who have been saying of late, 'What shall I do for the Lord?' And the word of the Lord would say unto thee, 'What thou shalt do for Me is this: thou shalt fall before Me until I make of thee a fire. Thou shalt not be destroyed, but thou shalt be consumed by my fire.' " And in that hour that long, lost call shall come to pass, for it is a new day.

And again I say unto you, It is easier for a camel to go through the eye of a needle, than for a rich man to enter into the kingdom of God. **Matthew 19:24**

Chapter Sixteen

The Parable of
The Eye of the Needle

I STOOD AMONG THE SONS OF men, strong and tall. My heart was filled with enthusiasm. My life was given to the purposes of God. Upon that day, I said to the Lord, "I will do mighty exploits in the name of my God."

The Lord came unto me, and He said, "What is it, son of man, that thou wouldst have?"

I said, "Lord, if I could only be among those who play sweetly upon an instrument and who sing well in the house of the Lord, then I would do great things for my God."

The Lord came to me, and He gave unto me the desire of my heart. He stood me among the sons of men. He let me play, and He let me sing. I saw the day when the hearts of men were moved by that thing that the Lord had given unto me.

After hearts of men were moved, I stood back, and I said to myself, "Now I will be content, for I have been able to move the hearts of men." But in my secret hour, I bowed my heart before my God and said, "Lord, Thou hast given what I asked for, but my heart is heavy. I have a longing for something more."

He came again unto me in the night season. He asked me again, "Son of man, ask Me again the thing that thou wouldst have of Me."

I said, "Lord, I see men bowed by burdens low. I see hearts that are broken. I see sadness and discouragement. O, give me the power of the spoken word that I might speak the Word and their hearts will be delivered."

The Lord came unto me and said, "Son of man, I have given thee the things which thou has desired."

With great joy, I marched before the people of God. In my youth and in my enthusiasm, I spoke the Word and men were delivered. I spoke the

The Parable of The Eye of the Needle

Word, and their hearts were made whole. I knew what it was to bind the brokenhearted and to pour in the oil of joy for mourning.

While men were praising Him and glorifying His name, I went back to my secret chamber. I bowed my head in sorrow. I said, "O my God, O my God. I am not satisfied."

He came again unto me and he said, "Son of man, what is it that thou again desirest of Me?"

And I said, "O my God, give me power in my hands that as Thou didst do, I might lay my hands upon the sick and see healing flow."

He said unto me, "It is done as thou has commanded."

From that very day, as I went to the nations of the Earth, I saw the sick raised from their sick beds. I saw pain and suffering go away.

I was rejoicing as I went to my secret place. I bowed my head before my God. I said, "Now, my God, I will be satisfied, for Thou has given me that which I have desired."

No sooner had the words come out of my mouth when the heart within me began to ache and cry. I said, "God, I do not understand this. Again my heart is sad." I said, "Lord, wilt Thou just one more time give me the thing I ask of Thee?"

He said, "It is done."

I said, "God, I desire to go against principalities

and powers, the powers of the wickedness of this world in spiritual darkness in high places."

He said, "Surely I give it unto thee. Now go."

So I went, and the Lord allowed me to go into dens of iniquity and holes and dives where men hide from the light because of the sin and evil that is upon them. There was a day when I saw demons cry out at the very presence of the power of God that rested.

Then I went back to my secret place broken. I said, "God, I have asked Thee for all that I desire, and still my heart is not satisfied. Nor do I feel that I have touched the thing that Thou hast called me to. In my youth I had expended myself with all the things that my heart had desired."

Then one more time a gracious and loving God visited me in the night season. He said, "Now, what is it that thou dost desire?"

In brokenness of heart, I bowed before Him, and I said, "God, only that thing which Thou dost desire to give unto me."

He came unto me and said, "Come with Me, and I will take thee on a journey." He took me past my friends. He took me past those with whom I had come into the house of the Lord. He took me into a desolate place. He caused me to go into a place alone in the wilderness.

The Parable of The Eye of the Needle

I said, "O my God, Thou hast cut me off from those I love. What art Thou doing unto me?"

He said, "I take thee to the place where all men must come if their heart's cry is to be fulfilled."

At a certain hour, I bowed before a gate that is called, "the Eye of the Needle." There before the Eye of the Needle I heard the voice of the Lord say, "Bow low." I bowed low. He said, "No, lower." So I bowed lower. He said, "Yet lower. Thou dost not go low enough." So I went as low as I could go.

I had upon my back my books of learning. I had with me my instruments of music. I had with me my gifts and abilities. He said unto me, "Thou hast too much, thou canst not go through this gate."

I said, "God, Thou hast given me these books. Thou hast given me these abilities."

He said, "Drop them, or thou dost not go." So I dropped them, and I went on through a very small gate that is called "the Eye of the Needle."

As I went through this gate, I heard the voice of the Lord say, "Now rise to the other side." As I rose, a very strange thing happened to me. For lo, the gate which was so small that I must lay aside everything, was so wide I could not fill it.

As I stood in the presence of the Lord, I said, "God, what is this thing that Thou hast done unto me, for my soul is now satisfied?"

He said, "Thou hast come through the gate of

worship. Now come up to the Circle of the Earth, and I will show thee a great mystery. I will reveal unto thee the thing that I am doing among the sons of men."

The Spirit of the Lord caught me away. He took me to the Circle of the Earth, higher than the eagle flies, beyond where the clouds can rumble, beyond where the sun shines or the moon finds her path. There at the throne of my God, He said, "Look down upon My people."

I saw strange things. I saw my companions gathered around a very small gate. I saw them wringing their hands and crying. They were saying to one another, "God hath given us these instruments of war. This sword is my sword, and I will work against the enemy. I will bring the enemy down. I cannot go through this gate, for if I go through this gate, I must put down my sword. God has called me to be a warrior, and therefore I will not do it."

And I heard another one say, "Me? Lay down my instruments of music? Lay down all that God has given unto me, just to go through that silly little gate, to be nothing but a bare man who comes out on the other side stripped of everything? I cannot do this thing!" I saw them as they stood aside in their pride, afraid to bow themselves before a very small gate.

The Parable of The Eye of the Needle

Then I saw again, as the Lord brought me closer to the gate, I saw a man bow low, laying down everything that he had. As he came through the very wide gate on the other side, his instruments of music were there. His sword was there. His books were there. The power was there.

The word of the Lord came to me, "Go now and tell this people before thee, I have given unto this people extreme talents and much ability. I have called those who are instrumentalists to play. But I say unto thee this day, if thou dost not come through the very small gate, which is the gate of worship, and bow low and lay before Me thine instruments, thy talents, thine abilities, thy vision, and thy power, thou shalt always be among those who will only be able to minister to the hearts of men and bless the hearts of men.

"But there is a gate open in the Church in this hour which is a very small gate. Through that gate only men who are worshippers will go. These men will lay talents before their God. These men will say 'God, we will be worshippers.' Through that wide gate they will come. As they come through that wide gate (hear again the Word of the Lord), they will arise again on the other side, not to minister unto men, but to minister unto their God.

"I now present before thee a choice. Thou canst

minister unto men, and I will cause thee to sway the hearts of men with thy talent. Or thou canst humble thyself as one passing through a very low gate and become a worshiper of God. Then thou shalt minister unto the King."

* This, the best known of her prophetic parables, was given by Dr. Baker at the 1981 National Worship Symposium in Dallas, Texas.

To the chief Musician, A Psalm for the sons of Korah. Hear this, all ye people; give ear, all ye inhabitants of the world: Both low and high, rich and poor, together. My mouth shall speak of wisdom; and the meditation of my heart shall be of understanding. I WILL INCLINE MINE EAR TO A PARABLE: I will open my dark saying upon the harp. Psalm 49:1-4

Notes

ॐ *Notes* ॐ

Notes

ଓଓ *Notes* ଓଓ

CB *Notes* BO

Notes